ANIMAL
TRUE RESCUE STORIES
HEROES

SANDRA MARKLE

M MILLBROOK PRESS • MINNEAPOLIS

From the Author

I wish that I could share with you what was a very special part of writing *Animal Heroes: True Rescue Stories*—listening to each person tell their story. As in my recent book, *Rescues!* these stories were amazing and inspiring, but this time there was an extra element. As each person talked about the animal or animals that had touched their life, they always expressed admiration and, when it had been a long-term relationship, love. I have to admit, more than once, I was moved to tears by what they had to say. And while the animal in my own life, my pet cat, Tiger, hasn't officially rescued me, I greatly value his companionship and appreciate that he's a part of my family.

FOR ALL THOSE SPECIAL ANIMALS THAT
MAKE OUR LIVES BETTER IN SO MANY WAYS.

Millbrook Press
A division of Lerner Publishing Group, Inc.
241 First Avenue North
Minneapolis, MN 55401 U.S.A.

Website address: www.lernerbooks.com

Library of Congress Cataloging-in-Publication Data

Markle, Sandra.
     Animal heroes : true rescue stories / by Sandra Markle.
        p. cm.
     Includes bibliographical references and index.
     ISBN 978-0-8225-7884-0 (lib. bdg. : alk. paper)
   1. Pets—Anecdotes—Juvenile literature. 2. Animals—Anecdotes—Juvenile literature. 3. Animal heroes—Anecdotes—Juvenile literature. I. Title.
   SF416.2.M266 2009
   636.088'7—dc22   2007050435

Manufactured in the United States of America
4 – MG – 11/1/10

CONTENTS

NO ONE KNOWS WHEN DISASTER MAY STRIKE.

A flood, a hurricane, or a terrorist attack suddenly puts people into terrifying situations. Sometimes people accidentally get themselves into trouble too. Either way, the danger is real. In this book, you will find dramatic, real-life stories of animal heroes. Some of the animals were trained to help others. Others just happened to be in the right place at the right time. These stories also show how people have learned to work with animals in ways that make the most of each animal's special abilities to help humans.

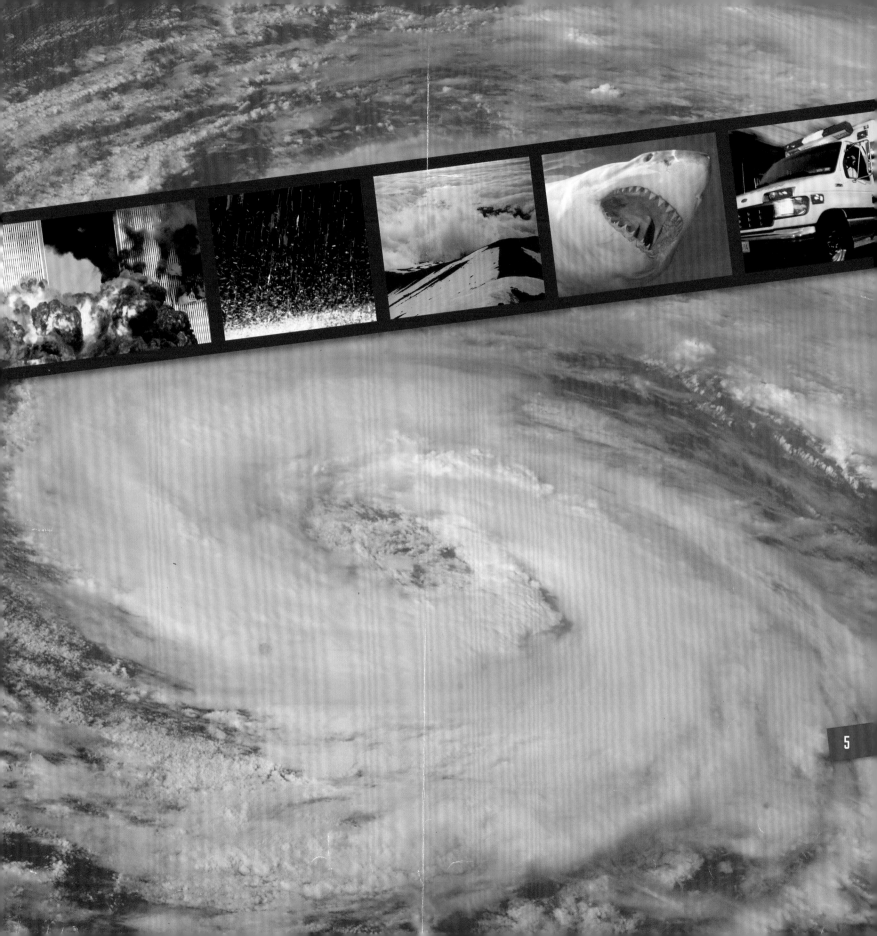

ROSELLE FINDS A WAY

6

TUESDAY STARTED OFF

like a normal workday for Mike Hingson. He worked on the seventy-eighth floor of Tower 1 (the North Tower) in the World Trade Center. Mike was the regional sales manager for a company providing computer data storage systems. He was leading a training program for his sales team. Suddenly, an explosion and the sound of screams interrupted his talk. The building shuddered, tilted, and then slowly righted itself.

Mike's friend, David Frank, shouted, "There's fire and smoke and a million pieces of paper falling past the window." Mike is blind. He couldn't see what David was describing. But he could hear the falling debris and the sounds of panicked people all around him. Mike sensed something else too. His guide dog Roselle, who was quick to respond to danger, had remained still. She was thumping her tail against his leg. So he shouted to his group, "Calm down. We're going to get out of here, but we've got to do it in an orderly way." Following his instructions, his coworkers walked rather than ran for the stairs.

7

American Airlines Flight 11 crashed into Tower 1 at 8:46 A.M. local time, striking the ninety-fourth through the ninety-eighth floors.

The Escape

Going down seventy-seven flights of stairs was a daunting task. Because of the noise and all the people on the stairs, Mike had to keep instructing Roselle to go forward. Roselle had to hold a steady pace that Mike could follow despite the crowds.

Mike smelled the odor of jet fuel burning and guessed a plane had struck Tower 1. He and the others had to stop and step aside to let rescuers carrying burn victims pass. The rescuers needed to rush them to the hospital as quickly as possible. Firefighters trudged by too, heading up the stairs with boots scuffling and heavy gear rustling. Mike and Roselle labored on, floor after floor, until they finally reached the exit.

Dave offered Mike a ride to his home in New Jersey. They walked toward the parking lot below Tower 2 (the South Tower). But as soon as David could see Tower 2, he reported it was burning as well. Then Mike heard a deep rumble, and someone yelled, "Get out of here! It's coming down!"

As workers walked down the stairs of Tower 1, firefighters headed up to fight the blaze.

WHO'S THE LEADER?

Dogs are naturally used to living in a group, or pack. In the pack, they accept one member as their leader. This natural behavior means a guide dog can also learn to follow instructions from a human leader. Mike said, "As the leader of our team, it's my job to give specific commands and to sound confident about what I'm telling Roselle to do." That, he admitted, was sometimes difficult during their escape from the World Trade Center. "But," he added, "I did it for Roselle, and keeping her focused helped me too."

Tower 2 *(left)* started to collapse at 9:59 A.M., after being struck by United Airlines Flight 175.

Still More Danger!

Mike turned away from the noise. He called to Roselle, "Go forward! Hop up!" It was her command to go faster. As Mike ran, guided by Roselle, the rumble became a monstrous noise chasing after them.

Then Mike was covered by a cloud of dust so thick he felt as though he was drowning in it. Roselle didn't panic. She kept guiding Mike straight ahead. They became separated from Dave in the rush. Desperate to escape the dust, Mike listened for the sound that signaled he was passing a doorway. The instant he heard it, he shouted, "Go right!" Roselle turned as ordered, but she went only a few steps before jerking to a stop.

People ran from a giant wave of dust and debris as Tower 2 collapsed.

Mike knew if Roselle stopped, she had a reason. He felt around with his foot and discovered he was at the top of a flight of stairs. The sounds and smells made him guess this was the entrance to one of New York's subway stations. He stayed there only briefly. Then he started walking along the street again.

After he had walked for a while, Mike heard the same horrible rumble as before. He guessed Tower 1 must be collapsing too. This time, though, he knew he was far enough away to be safe. So he stood with his back pressed against a building and Roselle against his legs until the roar became a whisper. Mike was shaken but determined to get home to his wife, Karen. He headed for New Jersey. Because none of the city's transportation systems were operating, Mike and Roselle had to walk for hours. Finally, Mike found a train that was running to New Jersey. He and Roselle reached home at seven that night.

Mike and Roselle

A huge cloud of smoke hung over New York after both towers of the World Trade Center collapsed.

11

GUIDE DOG IN TRAINING

Roselle was born in the Guide Dogs for the Blind kennel. Her training started when she was just eight weeks old. She went to live with a puppy raiser. This is a person who teaches guide dog puppies basic skills, such as to sit, to stay, and to be friendly to everyone they meet.

When she was about eighteen months old, Roselle's official training started. She returned to the school, where she lived in a kennel with lots of other dogs. She worked with a trainer to learn guide dog skills. These included walking in a straight line, stopping at curbs, and going up and down stairs at a slow, steady pace.

First, Roselle trained on a treadmill and became used to wearing a harness. Then she and her trainer took trips to a nearby town to practice. After about five months, Roselle was ready for her final exam. She had to follow voice commands to guide her blindfolded instructor through the test course. About 35 percent of guide dog trainees don't pass the test. Those dogs become house pets. Roselle graduated and went on to a long career as Mike's service partner.

Afterward

The skyline of New York City changed forever on September 11, 2001. The lives of the many people involved in the attacks changed as well. Mike went back to work. First, he worked from home and then in his company's new office space. Six months later, though, Mike changed jobs. He wanted to do something that helped people more directly. He became the director of National Public Affairs at Guide Dogs for the Blind. Mike travels around the country, sharing the story of his escape from the World Trade Center. With his story, he helps to raise money so that more dogs can be trained to help the blind. Roselle retired from her role as guide dog in 2007. She still lives with Mike and Karen as an important part of their family.

On September 11, 2001, Mike and Roselle worked as a team and depended on each other to stay safe.

MOTHER GORILLA SAVES TODDLER
BROOKFIELD, ILLINOIS, AUGUST 16, 1996

14

BINTI JUA, A FEMALE

western lowland gorilla, was sitting in the warm summer sunshine nursing her infant daughter Koola. Then a woman screamed. A three-year-old boy had tumbled over the railing into the Brookfield Zoo's rain forest exhibit.

A zoo visitor with a camera filmed what happened next. Before the seven other adult gorillas in the exhibit could react, Binti Jua placed her own infant on her back and rushed to the unconscious child. She picked him up and cradled him in one big arm.

Chris Demitros, lead keeper for the zoo's gorillas and other apes, grabbed his radio and called in a Signal 13. This is the zoo's code for a life-threatening emergency. He instructed his team to move the other gorillas to their indoor habitat and away from Binti.

No one knew what to expect when the mother gorilla picked up the young boy.

Gorilla on Guard

The keepers opened the door to the indoor habitat. Usually the gorillas would hurry inside because the open door meant that they would be fed. This time, the gorillas stayed in the outdoor pen. They watched Binti. But Binti was acting like a mother guarding her young, so they stayed away from her.

Finally, the keepers got out big hoses and sprayed streams of water at the gorillas. In response, they started moving toward the door. The keepers hoped to separate Binti from the group. But the mother gorilla followed the others. She carried the little boy with her. The child's mother and the zoo staff held their breaths. They wondered what Binti would do when she reached the door. Then, just before she left the rain forest exhibit, the mother gorilla laid the little boy gently on the floor. The zoo's security team rushed into the area. They closed the door to keep the gorillas from returning and took the child to a waiting ambulance. Fortunately, he had only a broken wrist and some minor cuts and bruises.

16

Zoo visitors look down into the gorilla habitat a few days after the toddler fell.

ZOOS HELP GORILLAS

Western lowland gorillas, like Binti, are listed as endangered. This means the number of gorillas living in their natural habitat, or home, is shrinking. They could be in danger of becoming extinct. Extinct means there would be no more of these animals alive. In the wild, western lowland gorillas live only

on the west coast of Africa. There, people are clearing the gorillas' natural habitat to make room for farms and homes.

To help western lowland gorillas survive, zoos around the world are working together in a breeding program. Scientists watching the gorillas in the wild learned these animals breed only when they live in groups. Each group has one dominant (lead) male, a number of females, and the group's young. Using this information, zoos moved adults to create social groups so that they would produce young. When those young become adults, the zoos move them to form new family groups. This plan helps ensure the western lowland gorillas survive, at least in zoos.

Afterward

Binti Jua's rescue made headlines around the world. She was awarded a medal from the American Legion and honorary membership in the California Parent-Teacher Association (PTA). Binti Jua still lives at the Brookfield Zoo. In 2006, she gave birth to a new baby, a male named Bakari. The boy who fell, a teenager now, doesn't remember the time a mother gorilla held him gently in her arms.

18

Binti cradles her napping baby, Bakari.

What is it with Mothers?

Scientists suspect the mothering instinct, the way Binti Jua behaved with the boy, is set off by certain hormones. Hormones are special chemicals in the body. Some are made after a female gives birth. This instinct can lead to amazing behavior.

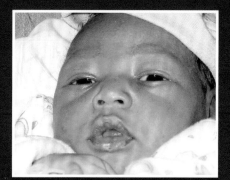

Baby Angel

Angel's rescuers

In 2005, a stray dog was foraging for food in the Ngong Forest near Nairobi, Kenya. It discovered an abandoned newborn human baby girl. The dog gently picked up the infant and carried her to the place it had left its own litter of pups. The baby was discovered by two children who heard the infant's cries. They ran to get their mother. Their mother took the baby girl to the Kenyatta National Hospital. The girl, whom the nurses named Angel, was soon adopted. The family that found the baby adopted the stray mother dog and her pups.

Writers have created stories, like *Tarzan of the Apes* by Edgar Rice Burroughs, about children living with animals. But there are also the rare true stories. In 1998 police in Moscow, Russia, discovered a six-year-old boy living on the streets with a pack of wild dogs. The police tried several times to capture the boy, but each time the dogs came to his defense and attacked. Finally, the police were able to rescue the boy. They sent him to live at a children's home. Later, the police learned the boy had escaped an abusive family when he was four. He lived by begging for food. Then he began to share what he got with a pack of dogs. The dogs adopted him and allowed him to live with them. They shared food with him and slept curled up around him during the winter to keep him warm.

Rain bucketed down

all day Sunday. It was still raining Monday morning when Kim Riley drove the tractor out to the pasture. She was bringing in the cows for milking. The Rileys' dairy farm was close to the Manawatu River gorge on the North Island of New Zealand. The Manawatu River flowed through this deep, narrow canyon. After so much heavy rain, the Manawatu was roaring through the canyon. As Kim approached the cows, she saw the river had flooded the pastures where they were grazing.

20

Almost at once, the tractor became stuck in the water and mud. Kim climbed off the tractor to herd the cows on foot. When some of the cows ran away from her, she chased after them. Kim saw several cows glide past her. She realized they were floating. And so was she! She had been afraid the cows would be swept away. Now she too was being carried along by the river.

Groups of cows huddled together wherever they could get out of the swift-flowing floodwaters.

Trapped!

Kim stretched out on her back. She thought she would float and kick her feet to get herself to solid ground. But her rubber boots had filled with water and dragged her feet down. She struggled to pull off the boots. Then she started swimming, but almost at once, the current tossed her into a big pile of weeds and sticks. The pile was also being swept along by the raging river.

No sooner did she get free of the debris than a cow ran into her, pushed her underwater, and swam over the top of her. As Kim surfaced, she gulped in some of the smelly, muddy water. Then she was dunked by another cow. "That was when I got scared," Kim admitted. "I knew I was still about half a mile [1 kilometer] away from the gorge, but I was getting tired and couldn't seem to escape the current." The gorge has sheer rock walls. If Kim was swept into it, she might be tossed against those rocks and be killed. Or she might become too tired to keep afloat and drown. She was running out of time to escape the river.

The flooding river damaged homes and roads. It also washed out this bridge.

Cow 569

Kim saw one cow peel off from a group swimming in circles as the river pulled them downstream. She paddled hard and swam to it. Kim recognized Cow 569. She knew this animal was strong-willed and pushy. Kim said, "I could see even now how determined she looked, and I figured she was going to make it out of the river." So Kim threw her arms around the cow's big neck and stretched out alongside her bulging side. Cow 569 grunted in annoyance. Still, she allowed Kim to hitch a ride to solid ground, nearly half the length of a football field away.

COWS FLOAT

Cows can easily float in water. The reason? Eating gives them gas. A cow's stomach is divided into four chambers. The first, called the rumen, is the biggest. It can hold as much as 66 gallons (250 liters) of food and water. In the rumen, plant material, such as the grass that the cow eats, mixes with bacteria. The bacteria begin to break down the grass into food nutrients. This process produces methane gas. As the cow continues to chew, this gas is released into the air. But the cow always has some gas in its rumen, giving it its own kind of inflated inner tube.

Afterward

Kim lay on the ground where she'd pulled herself ashore and rested briefly. Then she set off walking. Her worried husband, Keith, soon found her. About fifteen cows had been swept into the river. The Rileys never saw them again. But the rest of the herd survived, including Cow 569. Although she was exhausted, Kim was otherwise fine. The very next day, she was back helping with the farmwork.

Three years later, at the age of twelve, Cow 569 retired. Kim said, "Most retired dairy cows [are sent to the slaughterhouse to] become hamburgers, but not that one." In appreciation for rescuing Kim, the Rileys are allowing Cow 569 to live out her days doing what cows enjoy most, munching grass.

Kim gives Cow 569 a pat to say thanks.

GEORGE AND FRISKY SURVIVE KATRINA
BILOXI, MISSISSIPPI, AUGUST 29, 2005

People evacuating the Gulf Coast before Hurricane Katrina created huge traffic jams.

By Sunday, August 28, residents all along the Gulf of Mexico had fled inland. They were leaving areas in the path of approaching Hurricane Katrina. But George Mitchell stayed at home in Biloxi, Mississippi. He'd just celebrated his eightieth birthday and had weathered three hurricanes in Biloxi. He figured he could live through another one.

At the last minute, George did agree to move into the home of a friend and neighbor who had decided to leave. The friend's home was on higher ground than his. George's house and yard backed right onto Brashier Bayou close to Biloxi Bay. Being so close to water is especially dangerous because hurricanes can cause flooding. George took Frisky, his nineteen-year-old miniature poodle-schnauzer mix, with him. That evening, George and Frisky lay down on an inflated air mattress in the master bedroom of his friend's boarded-up house and went to sleep.

PETS FOR GOOD HEALTH

Scientific studies report that pet owners tend to be healthier than people without pets. No one is certain why. But medical tests show that people with pets generally tend to have lower blood pressure. Blood pressure is the force blood puts on the arteries and veins as it moves through them. Having lower blood pressure causes less strain on the body. Pet owners are happier with their lives, and this also helps them stay healthy.

Katrina Strikes!

At about 11 P.M., the sound of smashing glass woke George. He leaped up. The power had gone off, so he switched on a flashlight and went to check on the noise. He discovered a fence board poking through the bathroom window. It was the only window in the house that faced away from the bay and the only window that hadn't been boarded up. But that was just the beginning of the storm's rampage.

Raindrops pelted the house like a million tacks. Hearing a banging noise above the wind's roaring, George tracked the sound to the kitchen. As he arrived, the wind peeled off the flapping back door. In the vivid light cast by zigzagging lightning bolts, George saw trees bent nearly to the ground by the wind. Worse, dark water was surging toward the house.

Hurricane Katrina attacked with sustained winds of 125 miles (201 km) per hour.

HURRICANES

Hurricanes are Earth's biggest storm systems. They form over warm tropical oceans. When the surface water warms up enough, a lot of it evaporates, or turns into water vapor, and moves into the air. This warm, moist air quickly rises to where the air is cooler. There it forms thunderstorm clouds. A cluster of clouds merges to form a storm system. When the winds in this system blow steadily at 75 miles (120 km) per hour, the storm becomes a hurricane.

The satellite image shows Hurricane Katrina. The force of Earth's spinning is called the Coriolis force. It makes the hurricane winds turn, creating the pinwheel cloud pattern. In the center, warm, dry air surges downward. Then it pushes outward, creating the storm's eye. This is a center area of calm surrounded by a wall of clouds. The storm's winds are strongest around the eye.

Danger in the Water

The floodwaters poured into the house. "There was such a strong current," George said, "I felt like I was standing in a giant washing machine. And I could see fish swimming around my legs."

Because Frisky was so old, George was worried the dog would drown or be swept away. He put Frisky on the air mattress and kept a tight hold so it wouldn't tip over. Suddenly, George spotted two snakes, water moccasins, slithering across the surface of the water toward the floating air mattress—and Frisky. George struck one snake with his hand, flinging it through the bedroom doorway. The other snake disappeared underwater. George grabbed his flashlight. He shone it in one direction and then another, watching for the snakes.

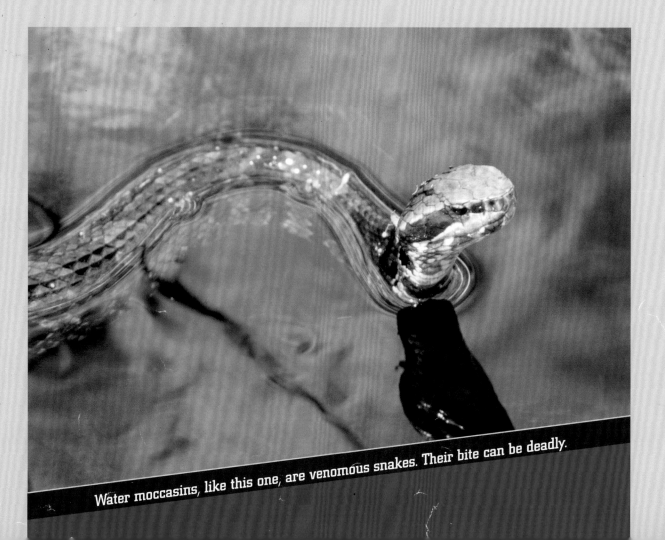

Water moccasins, like this one, are venomous snakes. Their bite can be deadly.

Frisky Doesn't Give Up

Although he didn't see the snakes again, George soon had something else to worry about—keeping his head above water. The water continued to surge through the house. Soon it was so deep, George was forced to tread water while he held onto the air mattress. Hour after hour, the water continued to rise until George's head was just below the room's ceiling. He was exhausted. He said, "I started to give up. Then Frisky crawled to the edge of the mattress and licked my face."

For the rest of the night, Frisky licked George every time he stopped treading water or let go of the mattress. Frisky's licks kept George awake and treading water. Finally, the water level in the house started to go down. At about noon on Monday, George was able to escape the house, carrying Frisky with him. He was shocked to see how badly the hurricane had damaged the neighborhood.

Hurricane Katrina damaged an estimated 90 percent of the homes and businesses along the Biloxi-Gulfport coastline.

Afterward

George was taken to the hospital for observation. Frisky went with him. The nurses and doctors decided it was only fair that the pair that had kept each other alive should stay together.

George's neighborhood was badly damaged. The combined forces of wind and water had caused many problems. Trees were uprooted, windows broken, roofs ripped off, and even whole houses were destroyed. George's friend's house, where he rode out the storm, could be repaired. George's own home though had to be torn down. After getting out of the hospital, George moved into a retirement home. Of course, Frisky went with him there too.

For George, Frisky isn't just a pet—he's family.

DOG WARMS LOST HIKERS
Mount Hood, Oregon, February 18, 2007

IT WAS JUST SUPPOSED TO BE AN OVERNIGHT HIKE

on Mount Hood, Oregon's highest peak. The eight friends had chosen a gently sloping route. So when the group set out on Saturday morning, Matt Bryant took along his dog, Velvet, a Labrador-cattle dog mix. According to plan, the group hiked, dug a snow cave, and spent the night on the mountain. Sunday the group planned to climb higher. But the weather forced a change of plans. Mount Hood was covered by a fierce snowstorm.

Freezing, hurricane-force winds roared and whipped snow in every direction. The hikers' only goal was to get off the mountain safely. They could see no more than arm's length in front of them, so they formed two groups. Each held onto a safety line that connected the hikers in that group. To keep Velvet from getting lost, Matt clipped her collar onto the safety line directly behind him. Since there were just four clips to a line, the fourth person in Matt's group, Trevor Liston, only held onto the line.

Matt was an experienced climber, familiar with Mount Hood. He led the way with Velvet and the three others behind him. Because he was nearly blinded by the snow, though, he had to lead by reading his compass. He headed in the direction he knew should take them back the way they'd come the day before. To avoid tripping over any snow-buried rocks, he kept tapping the ground in front of him with a ski pole.

Winter storms pose serious dangers for hikers on Oregon's Mount Hood.

The group had nearly 2 miles (3.2 km) to hike to retrace their steps. They hoped they would eventually walk out of the storm. Instead, the weather grew steadily worse. Soon they were walking through a whiteout. The milky white swirling snow was so thick it was impossible to tell the sky from the ground or one direction from another.

The Big Fall

Suddenly, the ground dropped out from under Matt's feet. "I was falling. Then I was sliding on ice," Matt said. "I tried to flip over to stop myself but couldn't. I wondered if I was going to die."

Seconds and nearly 500 feet (150 meters) later, Matt skidded to a surprisingly gentle stop at the bottom of a canyon. He had twisted his ankle, but he was otherwise uninjured. Trevor had let go of the rope and was pulled to safety by someone in the other group. Velvet and Kate Hanlon bumped to a stop behind Matt and were also unhurt. Then Christina Redl crashed down and lay unconscious. She was bleeding from a deep gash on her head.

Lost!

Christina quickly regained consciousness. Kate was able to stop the bleeding, but her friend was weak and dazed. Her pack had been lost in the fall. With Matt and Kate helping her, the group started walking again. Matt figured they could walk out of the canyon and find help. And less than an hour later, the storm eased. Luckily, it cleared a little just in time for them to discover they were walking straight toward another cliff. The trio decided they had no choice but to hunker down and wait to be rescued. Rock-hard, wind-scoured ice covered the canyon floor. It was too hard to dig into it to make a snow cave for shelter. At least Matt and Kate still had their packs and camping gear. They spread out their two ground cover sleeping pads side by side. They zipped their sleeping bags into one big blanket and topped this off with their one plastic tarp. Then, as the daylight faded and the storm intensified again, Matt, Kate, Christina, and Velvet crawled into their makeshift shelter.

HYPOTHERMIA AND FROSTBITE

Hypothermia is what happens to the human body when the core temperature, the temperature of the internal body organs, drops well below normal. First, the person shivers severely, then fingers and toes become numb, and movement becomes difficult. As chilling continues, organs inside the body stop working. The person may die.

When body parts, like toes and fingers, become frozen, it is called frostbite. The skin and tissue under the skin can be damaged. If the frostbite was severe and the tissue is dead, the frostbitten part will have to be removed. To avoid frostbite, people need to dress warmly and cover exposed parts of the body.

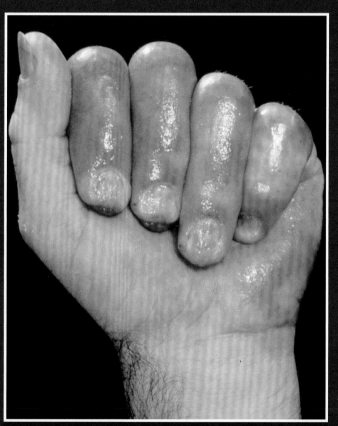

Frostbitten fingers become red and swollen.

Velvet to the Rescue

As night settled in, the temperature dropped. Even though they were huddled together, the hikers worried about becoming dangerously chilled. That's when Velvet came to their rescue. A dog has a body temperature of about 101°F (38.°C), a little warmer than a healthy human's temperature of 98.6F° (37°C). Velvet also had a thick fur coat to conserve her body heat. She stretched out on top of Matt, Christina, and Kate in turn to help them keep warm. Sometimes, she curled up by their feet, keeping their toes from freezing.

A couple of hours after taking refuge, Matt remembered something important. That morning, Christina had transferred her cell phone from her pack to her pocket. It hadn't been lost with her pack. He dialed 911 and got an answer. He reported they were alive and waiting to be rescued.

Besides the cell phone, the hikers were equipped with another important device, a Mountain Locator Unit. Matt had switched this on earlier. It was already transmitting a radio signal that searchers could use to find their location.

The lost hikers didn't know that their five friends had made it safely down the mountain and raised an alarm. Although the storm was too fierce for helicopters to help, the county sheriff's department was already launching a ground search.

A team of rescuers geared up and set off to search for the lost hikers.

MLU and PLB: How They Work

A Mountain Locator Unit (MLU) is a device used only on Mount Hood. It's a simple transmitter that sends only a radio signal. It's similar to the kind scientists use on radio collars to track animals. The Mount Hood rescue teams use an antenna to home in on the transmitter's signal. The signal strengthens as the antenna approaches the point from which the MLU is transmitting. The signal weakens as the antenna moves past that point.

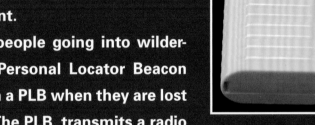

In other places, people going into wilderness areas carry a Personal Locator Beacon (PLB). People turn on a PLB when they are lost or need assistance. The PLB transmits a radio signal that's picked up by a low-orbiting satellite. A satellite is a device launched into orbit around Earth that is capable of both receiving signals from Earth and transmitting signals back to Earth. Satellite monitoring stations around the world watch for PLB transmissions and notify search and rescue authorities when a PLB has been turned on. Each PLB is registered to a specific owner. When a monitoring station receives a report, it carries a digital message of the PLB owner's identity, so searchers know who they're looking for.

The PLB transmitter also emits a signal similar to the one transmitted by the MLU. Some models include a GPS (global positioning system) unit. The signal is picked up by a network of satellites and their ground stations. This makes it possible to identify the location of the beacon within an area as small as a 32-foot (10 m) square. With this information, rescuers can reach a person who needs help much more quickly than in the past.

Search and Rescue

Despite the storm, the search for the lost hikers continued throughout the night. Teams trekked along the canyon rim, carrying their special antenna. Whenever they picked up the beacon's radio signal, they called in their compass reading to the search command post. This reading was marked on a map, and a line was drawn to extend across the canyon. When three lines crossed one another on the map, the searchers knew they had found the general location of the beacon.

At daybreak the next morning, four men from the Portland Mountain Rescue team walked into the canyon to search the area that had been pinpointed the night before. They took along an antenna to help them home in on the beacon's signal. Finally, at about 11 A.M., they found the hikers and Velvet huddled beneath their covers. Almost twenty hours after plunging into White River Canyon, the lost hikers were rescued. Matt said, "Thanks to Velvet none of us was suffering from hypothermia or frostbite."

Happy to be safe, Matt and Velvet head for home.

Afterward

Christina Redl suffered a concussion, a brain injury caused by a blow to the head, during the fall. She made a complete recovery. Kate Hanlon and Matt Bryant soon recovered from their minor injuries. Matt and Velvet returned to work. Matt works with children having behavior problems in Oregon's North Clackamas School District. The children earn points for good behavior so they can spend time with Velvet. Velvet is a trained therapy dog. Because of her gentle nature and training, she patiently accepts the children's attention and rewards them with licks and nuzzles. In 2008, Velvet received the American Red Cross Animal Award for the Breakfast of Champions Awards.

Matt and Velvet

WINNIE THE CAT SAVES HER FAMILY

NEW CASTLE, INDIANA, MARCH 24, 2007

IT WAS ONE O'CLOCK

in the morning. Cathy Keesling was sound asleep when the family's tabby cat, Winnie, jumped on her. Winnie meowed and pawed at her ear. Cathy woke up for a moment but quickly fell back asleep. Winnie meowed even louder. When Cathy woke up this time, she tried to awaken her husband, Eric. She couldn't rouse him and realized something was wrong. She dialed 911.

Next, Cathy staggered out of the bedroom to check on their fourteen-year-old son, Michael. She discovered him unconscious on the hallway floor. Minutes later, police and paramedics arrived. They immediately gave Cathy, Michael, and Eric 100 percent oxygen to breathe and rushed the family to the hospital.

Michael and Cathy revived quickly. Eric took more time. The family was lucky to survive. Later, they discovered that carbon monoxide, an odorless but deadly gas, had been the cause of their problems.

Eric had borrowed a gasoline-powered water pump to empty their flooded basement. The pump had a hole in the exhaust line. Exhaust fumes leaked out the hole. These fumes included carbon monoxide. The house was closed up tight for the winter, so the gas built up until it reached a dangerous level.

STARVED FOR OXYGEN

The problem with breathing carbon monoxide is that human red blood cells *(right)* pick up this gas more quickly than oxygen. Red blood cells usually carry oxygen throughout the body. We need this oxygen to live. When the blood delivers carbon monoxide instead, the body becomes oxygen starved. Headache, dizziness, and nausea are early symptoms. These are followed by unconsciousness and finally death.

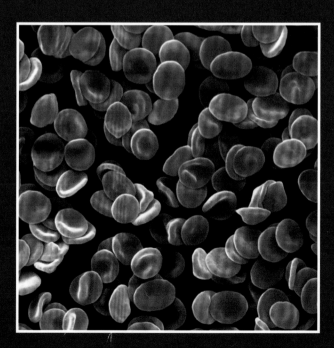

The Keesling family was treated by breathing in 100 percent oxygen for about five hours. It took that long for their body oxygen levels to return to normal. Winnie was fine and needed no treatment. Meanwhile, members of the fire department removed the faulty gasoline-powered pump from the Keesling's home. They set up huge fans inside the house to clear out the dangerous gas.

Afterward

The Centers for Disease Control and Prevention reports that, in the United States alone, as many as two hundred people a year die from carbon monoxide poisoning. By waking Cathy, Winnie saved the family and became a hero. In November 2007, the American Society for the Prevention of Cruelty to Animals (ASPCA) honored Winnie. She received a trophy and was named Cat of the Year. Winnie, though, was probably more pleased with the treat Cathy gave her—a whole fried chicken breast.

Winnie with her family, Eric (*left*), Cathy (*middle*), and Michael (*right*). Winnie has on a cape Cathy made for her to wear when she received her award.

Shark Attack!

It started out

as just a fun swim for the New Zealand lifeguard trainees. They were Nicola Howes, fifteen; Karina Cooper, fifteen; and Helen Slade, sixteen. Nicola's dad, veteran lifeguard Rob Howes, went along with the girls. When they were well beyond the breaking waves, seven dolphins suddenly surrounded them.

43

Dolphins with a Purpose

These were short-beaked common dolphins. The largest adults were nearly 8 feet (2.4 m) long and likely weighed more than 200 pounds (90 kilograms). Seeing dolphins at Ocean Beach and even swimming with them was pretty normal. But the behavior of this particular pod, or group, was anything but normal. Dolphins usually approached swimmers slowly and did not get too close to them. These dolphins arrived unexpectedly and began circling. Soon they were less than an arm's length away from the swimmers. Although they never brushed against Rob and the girls, the dolphins' ever-smaller circles forced the swimmers into a tight group. Rob said, "It was such bizarre behavior, the girls were screaming with fright. And I didn't know what to make of it either."

The dolphins circled closely, trapping the swimmers.

DOLPHINS AND PORPOISES

Dolphins and porpoises are not two names for the same creature. They are two different kinds of animals. Porpoises are usually smaller than dolphins. They are rarely more than 7 feet (2 m) long. Most kinds of dolphins are longer—some are over 10 feet (3 m) long. Dolphins have a slimmer body than porpoises, and they have a curved dorsal (upper back) fin. The plumper porpoises usually have a triangular dorsal fin. The final difference is that dolphins look as if they have a beak. Porpoises lack this pointed nose.

dolphin

porpoise

Rob knew for certain they needed help. His spirits rose when he spotted the lifeguard's boat in the distance. But the guards aboard it thought that Rob's waves were just a friendly greeting. The boat continued its patrol along the beach.

Suddenly, the circling dolphins began to leap and slap the water with their tails. Rob was now sure that he and the girls were in danger. He just didn't know whether the threat was from the dolphins or from something else.

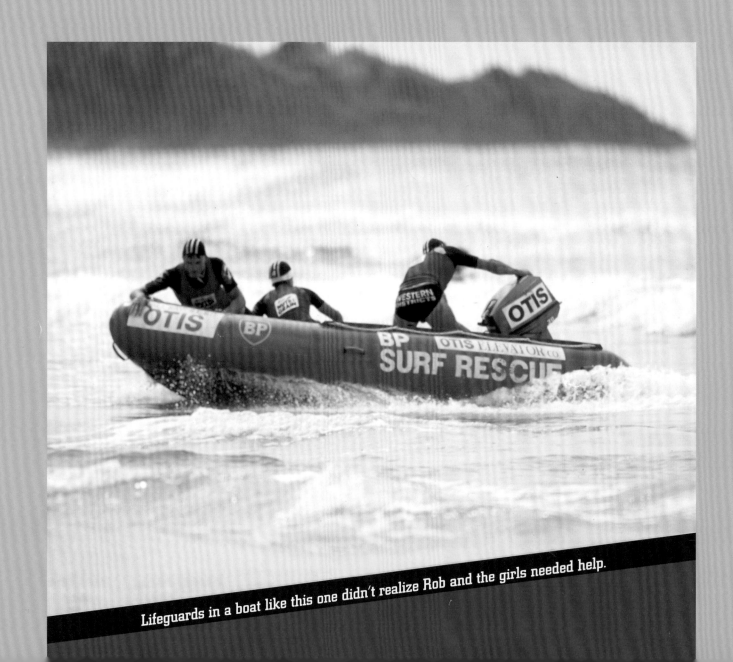

Lifeguards in a boat like this one didn't realize Rob and the girls needed help.

Dolphin Lifeguard

After being trapped by the circling dolphins for nearly forty minutes, Rob decided to make a break for it. He wanted to be able to look back and see if he could tell why the dolphins were acting so strangely. He also wanted to be able to clearly signal for help. He watched for his chance and, paddling hard, broke through the ring of circling dolphins. Then one of the dolphins peeled away from the others and charged straight toward Rob.

The dolphin submerged. Fearful of being struck from below, Rob tried to estimate where the dolphin would resurface. He turned and looked down into the water in that direction. What Rob saw next shocked him. No more than 6 feet (2 m) below him, a great white shark turned to get out of the way of the fast-swimming dolphin. Rob said. "I'll never forget watching that shark's long sleek, pale gray body glide past for what seemed like the longest time."

When Rob broke free, one of the dolphins chased after him.

DOLPHINS AND SHARKS

Stories about dolphins protecting people from sharks are not new, but only rarely are there witnesses who can verify this behavior. Usually dolphins take advantage of being part of a pod to avoid a shark encounter. The group in the pod has lots of eyes to watch out for approaching predators, like great whites. When one dolphin sees danger, like an approaching great white, it alerts the others and they swim away as fast as they can. A number of dolphins have bite-mark scars. These scars show that dolphins don't always swim fast enough.

Rob believes the great white had been tracking him and the girls as they swam along the shore. Great whites have keen senses that are always on the alert for prey. The shark may have first heard the swimmers' splashes and decided the sound indicated prey. Sharks can hear an animal moving in the water as far away as the length of a football field.

Luckily, the great white didn't attack. A great white's jaws are armed with nearly one hundred 2-inch (5-centimeter) long, razor-sharp teeth.

Suddenly, Rob realized that the dolphins had been acting to protect him and the girls from the hunting shark. As soon as the great white had passed Rob, the dolphins stopped splashing. They circled the girls a couple more times and then swam away.

Afterward

Despite this experience, Rob and the three girls are still active in the surf lifesaving program. Great white sharks regularly pass Ocean Beach. They are on their way to breed in the Hauraki Gulf, an area off the east coast of New Zealand's North Island. Rob has never again seen a shark quite so close, though. He hopes he never does.

Nicola Howes and her dad, Rob Howes, continue to enjoy spending time at Ocean Beach.

Tuffy, Lifeguard Of the Deep
Seafloor off California, 1965

The United States Navy wanted to find out if

humans could live and work deep underwater for long periods of time. So from 1964 through 1969, they built three special deepwater habitats: SEALAB I, II, and III. Teams of men (women weren't involved until later in the 1970s) lived in these undersea homes. They could work in the lab and go out of it to work underwater. They didn't need to surface for weeks at a time. While underwater, the SEALAB divers tested new tools and studied ocean life. Their experiments with a dolphin, Tuffy, proved dolphins and humans can work together deep underwater.

Tuffy at Work

Tuffy was a dolphin that worked as a lifeguard for the U.S. Navy's SEALAB II. In 1965, the Navy lowered SEALAB II to the seafloor off the coast of California, 203 feet (62 m) below the surface. Scott Carpenter had been one of the original NASA astronauts and the United States' fourth man in space. He spent thirty days in SEALAB II. Whenever he or other divers worked outside the lab, Tuffy was on duty.

Carpenter said, "We worked without a tether [rope] and couldn't see very far once we got even a little ways away from SEALAB's lights. So we wore a buzzer to call Tuffy if we got into trouble." Upon hearing the buzzer, Tuffy grabbed a line attached to the SEALAB and carried it to the diver. The diver could then follow the line back to the safety of the underwater habitat. Tuffy also wore a harness and divers could attach objects to it. Tuffy helped the divers by carrying tools, mail, and other supplies from the surface to the seafloor.

Unlike people, dolphins are able to quickly move from shallow water to deep water and back again without suffering any serious side effects. People who move too quickly between deep and shallow water develop a very painful condition called the bends.

When a diver pushed a buzzer, Tuffy swam to the rescue.

The Bends

If you've ever lifted a stack of books, you know the taller the stack, the heavier it is. Just like a stack of books, water has weight. When swimmers dive underwater, the pressure of the whole stack of water above them pushes down on their body. People are limited to how deep they can go because the pressure on their bodies becomes too great. Divers who stay underwater for any length of time breathe using the pressurized air stored in scuba tanks. While divers are deep underwater, the water pressure causes some of the gas in the air they breathe from the scuba tanks to dissolve into their blood and body tissue. If they surface slowly, their body absorbs this gas. If the diver surfaces too quickly, the gas remains as bubbles in the blood or collects in joints. This is the bends, and it can be very painful. It can even be fatal.

Why Don't Dolphins Get the Bends?

Dolphins don't get the bends because they don't breathe underwater. Dolphins are able to hold their breath much longer than people—sometimes as long as thirty minutes. They don't have to breathe pressurized air to stay underwater. For this reason, bubbles don't form in their blood. Scientists have observed dolphins breathing out before they dive. This removes most of the air in their lungs and gives the dolphins another advantage. As the water pressure increases, a dolphin's lungs can collapse without being damaged.

Heart Attack!

Plano, Texas, October 1996

JUST AFTER 5 a.m., Nancy Lingenfelter was awakened by Dakota's urgent nudges. She realized at once that the golden retriever was trying to signal that her husband, Mike, was having another heart attack. Nancy quickly called for an ambulance, and paramedics rushed him to the hospital.

53

Heart attacks were nothing new for Mike. He'd had his first heart attack five years earlier. Although he'd had heart surgery, Mike still had heart trouble. His heart muscle was so weakened that he continued to have heart attacks without warning. He also had a condition called angina. At times, part of Mike's heart didn't receive enough blood. This pain could be so intense that it caused Mike to black out. Mike always carried special medication to take at the start of an angina attack. Doctors told him that the medicine worked best taken just before an attack. But Mike had no warning symptoms, so he didn't know when he needed to take the medicine. Then Dakota came into his life.

HEART BYPASS SURGERY

To function properly, the heart, like the body's other organs, needs a supply of blood. Blood carries oxygen and food nutrients. The heart has its own set of blood vessels, called coronary arteries, to supply the blood it needs. About 5 percent of the blood the heart pumps goes through the coronary arteries. These arteries may become partly or even completely blocked by a buildup of fatty material. People with this problem can experience angina. These chest pains happen when people are active. Angina occurs when the heart needs to work harder but is not able to receive enough blood to do the job.

Doctors perform bypass surgery to help treat angina. The surgeon removes healthy blood vessels from another part of the patient's body, such as a leg, and attaches them to the heart. The healthy blood vessels let blood flow around blocked portions of coronary arteries. The increased blood flow to the heart helps it work better.

Dog Alarm

Mike's doctor suggested that having a dog might help Mike focus on something besides his heart condition. One of Nancy's friends gave him Dakota. Dakota had been rescued after being left chained in a backyard without food or water. At first, Mike resented having to take care of Dakota and walk him. But Mike discovered he felt better when he got out of the house and exercised. Soon he began to look forward to spending time with the dog. Then, to Mike's and Nancy's surprise, Dakota helped Mike in another way. Just before Mike had one of his unexpected angina attacks, Dakota started barking. He also nudged Mike to get his attention. After this happened several times, Mike realized Dakota's behavior was a signal for him to take his medication.

Mike said, "No one could figure out whether it was something about me that looked different or smelled different to Dakota, but he was always right. So I learned to take my medicine and lie down as soon as Dakota warned me." Dakota's warning kept Mike from blacking out, and the early dose of medicine made the angina attacks shorter and less painful. Dakota also helped Mike in another way. Once the angina pains started, Dakota would lie with his back against Mike's chest. The dog's body heat and slow, steady breathing helped keep Mike calm. Keeping calm helped to make Mike's attacks less severe too.

Dakota traveled everywhere with Mike.

Dakota helped Mike so much that he became a registered service dog. Service dogs have been trained to help people with disabilities or special needs. Guide dogs for the blind are the best known service dogs. Others alert deaf people to sounds, pull people in wheelchairs or, as in Mike's case, help people deal with health problems. In the United States, service dogs can stay with the person they're helping wherever they go—even in places that don't allow dogs. Dakota stayed close to Mike twenty-four hours a day. He went to work with Mike, to restaurants, and even along in the passenger cabin on airlines. Dakota helped other people too. He went with Mike to visit patients in hospitals. His friendly nature always seemed to make everyone he met feel better.

Dakota always seemed to know which patients needed his special attention.

Afterward

The Delta Society named Dakota 1999 Service Dog of the Year. This organization is devoted to animal-assisted therapy. Dakota was also elected to the Texas Veterinary Medical Foundation Animal Hall of Fame and the Alabama Hall of Fame. He was the first nonhuman to receive the Humanitarian of the Year award presented by the National Sertoma Club of Dallas. In 2001 Dakota developed heart problems of his own and died. While Mike misses Dakota, he feels fortunate to have another service dog, a golden retriever named Ogilvie. As a puppy, Ogilvie was trained by being with Dakota and Mike. It is Ogilvie's turn to help Mike prepare for future angina attacks.

As a pup, Ogilvie received on-the-job training from Dakota.

HELPING PAWS

Craig Cook has a very special service partner—a twenty-five-year old female capuchin monkey named Minnie. In 1996, when he was thirty years old, Craig was in a car accident that left him a quadriplegic, someone whose arms and legs don't work properly. Craig is unable to use his legs at all, and he can lift his arms just a little bit. For several years, Craig needed help from other people for such basic needs as getting a drink of water. Then Minnie came to Craig through the Helping Hands Organization.

Minnie was born at Southwick's Zoo in Mendon, Massachusetts, as part of the special Helping Hands program. While she was a baby, she was given to a foster family who cared for her and helped her learn to live with people. Like other Helping Hands monkeys in training, Minnie stayed with her foster family for twelve years. She learned basic skills such as obeying rules about what she could and couldn't touch and fetching things on command.

Next, Minnie attended the Helping Hands Monkey College for two years. At the college, she learned tasks that would help a handicapped person. These included taking food out of a refrigerator, putting a straw into a bottle, turning pages in a book one at a time, and picking up objects that had been dropped. It is a long training process, but capuchin monkeys can live to be forty-five years old. So they can be counted on to provide service for

many years. Best of all, monkeys like Minnie make a huge difference in people's lives.

Craig said, "Living with Minnie is like living with a good friend. And since she's been with me, Minnie's learned even more neat things to do, like make popcorn in the microwave. Thanks to Minnie, I can live independently with caregivers only coming in for a short time each day. And, when I go out, instead of being seen as the guy in the wheelchair, I'm now the guy with the monkey. How cool is that?"

AS ALL OF THE STORIES SHOW,

animals can make the difference when people face dangerous situations. Sometimes, animals even save a person's life. Animals can also make a difference in the quality of people's lives. They do this by providing special assistance or by encouraging people and strengthening their will to survive. In many different ways, animals can become heroes and help people face and overcome amazing challenges.

GLOSSARY

angina: pain due to some part of the heart not receiving enough oxygen-rich blood

bacteria: microscopic organisms. Bacteria in cow's stomachs help break down grass into food.

carbon monoxide: a poisonous, odorless gas that can be found in the exhaust of gasoline engines

Coriolis force: the result of the rotation of Earth. It makes storms rotate counterclockwise in the Northern Hemisphere and clockwise in the Southern Hemisphere.

debris: the broken remains of an object or objects

endangered species: a kind of plant or animal that is threatened with extinction, meaning that no more will exist

evacuating: removing people in danger

extinct: a plant or animal that is no longer in existence

gorge: a canyon or steep-sided valley, often with a river running through it

guide dog: a dog especially trained to help someone with a disability

hurricane: a powerful storm system made up of spiraling bands of thunderstorms with wind speeds of more than 74 miles (119 km) per hour

hypothermia: the condition of the body when its core temperature drops below normal

instinct: an inborn pattern of behavior

mothering instinct: the natural pattern of behavior that causes a mother to care for and protect her offspring

red blood cells: one of the main types of cells in blood. Red blood cells carry oxygen throughout the body.

rumen: the largest chamber of a cow's stomach

service animal: an animal trained to assist someone with a disability

SOURCE NOTES

Mike Hingson, telephone interview with author, January 31, 2007, 7, 10.

Craig Demitros, telephone interview with author, February 9, 2007, 15.

Kim Riley, telephone interview with author, February 1, 2007, 22, 23, 24.

George Mitchell, telephone interview with author, February 7, 2007, 29, 30.

Matt Bryant, telephone interview with author, November 27, 2007, 34, 38.

Rob Howes, telephone interview with author, February 2, 2007, 44, 47.

Scott Carpenter, telephone interview with author, February 16, 2007, 51.

Mike Lingenfelter, telephone interview with author, February 8, 2007, 55.

Craig Cook, telephone interview with author, February 23, 2007, 58, 59.

SELECTED BIBLIOGRAPHY

TELEPHONE INTERVIEWS WITH AUTHOR

Bryant, Matt, November 27, 2007.

Carpenter, Scott, February 16, 2007.

Cook, Craig, February 23, 2007.

Demitros, Craig, February 9, 2007.

Giesege, Claire, February 16, 2007.

Rocky Henderson, November 30, 2007.

Hingson, Michael, January 31, 2007.

Howes, Rob, February 2, 2007.

Keppeler, Megan, February 22, 2007.

Keesling, Cathy, and Eric Keesling, November 29, 2007.

Lingenfelter, Mike, February 8, 2007.

Mitchell, George, February 7, 2007.

Ridgway, Samuel, March 2, 2007.

Riley, Kim, February 1, 2007.

BOOKS

Lingenfelter, Mike, and David Frei. *The Angel by My Side*. Carsbad, CA: Hay House, 2002.

Ridgway, Sam. *Dolphin Doctor*. San Diego: Dolphin Science Press, 1995.

Riley, Kim. *Cow Power*. Auckland, NZ: Random House, 2004.

WEBSITES

Roselle Finds a Way

"Michael Hingson and his Guide Dog Roselle." *Guide Dogs for the Blind*. n.d. http://www.guidedogs.com /site/PageServer?pagename=programs_community _speakers _hingson (March 25, 2008).

Mother Gorilla Saves Toddler

"Binti Jua." *Wikipedia, the free encyclopedia*. March 11, 2008. http://en.wikipedia.org/wiki/Binti_Jua (March 25, 2008).

Cow 569 to the Rescue

"Cow Saves NZ Farmer from Floods." *BBC*. February 18, 2004. http://news.bbc.co.uk/2/hi/asia-pacific /3498871.stm (March 25, 2008).

George and Frisky Weather the Storm

"Biloxi Takes Stock of What Remains." *The Washington Post*. August 31, 2005. http://www .washingtonpost.com/wp-dyn/content/video/2005 /08/31/VI2005083101914.html (March 25, 2008).

"Old Dog Saves Owner from Katrina: George Mitchell Recounts How Trusty Dog Frisky Helped Him." *CBS News*. September 9, 2005. http://www .cbsnews.com/stories/2005/09/09/earlyshow /main829572.shtml (March 25, 2008).

Dog Warms Lost Hikers

"Velvet Received Hero Award." *Flickr*. March 11, 2008. http://www.flickr.com/photos/redcrosspdx /23267521/ (March 25, 2008).

Winnie the Cat

"Cat Saves Family from Poisonous Fumes." *MSNBC*. April 9, 2007. http://www.msnbc.msn.com /id/17972624 /?GTI=9246 (March 25, 2008).

Shark Attack!

Mercer, Phil. "Dolphins Prevent NZ Shark Attack." *BBC News*. November 23, 2004. http://news.bbc.co .uk/2/hi/asia-pacific/4034383.stm (March 25, 2008).

Tuffy, Lifeguard of the Deep

"People Under the Sea: Habitats." *Office of Naval Research*. n.d. http://www.onr.navy.mil/focus /blowballast/people/habitats1.htm (March 25, 2008).

Heart Attack

"Dog Saves Man from Heart Attack." *Dogsinthenews. com*. February 13, 2001. http://dogsinthenews.com /issues/0102/articles /010213a.htm (March 25, 2008).

Helping Paws

Wahle, Scott. "Monkey Helpers for the Disabled." *WBZtv.com*. January 17, 2006. http://wbztv.com /specialreports/local_story _004211942.html (March 25, 2008).

To find out even more, check out the following books and websites.

BOOKS

Crisp, Marty. *Everything Dolphin: What Kids Really Want to Know about Dolphins*. Kids Faqs series. Chanhassen, MN: Northword Press, 2004.
Explore the basics about dolphin life and behavior plus more unusual facts, such as why dolphins appear to be smiling.

Kent, Deborah. *Animal Helpers for the Disabled*. Watts Library series. Danbury, CN: Franklin Watts, 2003. Discover how dogs help people as guides, service partners, and companions.

Markle, Sandra. *Can You Believe? Hurricanes*. New York: Scholastic, 2002. Explore why hurricanes form, how they are tracked, and ways scientists are working to help people stay safe.

Markle, Sandra. *Great White Sharks*. Animal Predators series. Minneapolis: Carolrhoda, 2004. Follow the great white on a hunt, and learn about how this animal is suited for its life as a top predator.

Markle, Sandra. *Rescues!*: Mineapolis: Millbrook Press, 2006. Exciting stories of people rescuing people.

Patent, Dorothy Hinshaw. *Right Dog for the Job: Ira's Path from Service Dog to Guide Dog*. New York: Walker, 2004. Photo essay follows a puppy through its training to become a guide dog for the blind.

Stewart, Kelly. *Gorillas*. World Life Library series. New York: Harper Trophy, 2003. The author studied wild mountain gorillas while an assistant to Dian Fossey, noted gorilla researcher, in Rwanda. Read about the gorillas social behavior, life history, and conservation efforts to protect gorillas.

WEBSITES

Animal Heroes
http://www.myhero.com/myhero/go/directory/directory.asp?dir=animal
Learn the true stories of animal heroes.

K-9 Heroes Remembered
http://www.uswardogs.org/id16.html
Read about dogs who helped soldiers during wartime.

InDex

The images in this book are used with the permission of: © APN/Mark Mitchell, pp. 1 (left), 21, 24; AP Photo/Tina Fineberg, pp. 1 (second from left), 40, 42; © Michael Sharkey, pp. 1 (center), 31; Melanie Stetson Freeman / © 2005 The Christian Science Monitor (www.csmonitor.com). All rights reserved, pp. 1 (second from right), 58, 59 (bottom); © Flip Nicklin/Minden Pictures, pp. 1 (right), 44, 47; © Tom Kates, Helping Hands, p. 4; NASA, pp. 5 (background), 28; © Spencer Platt/Getty Images, pp. 5 (left), 9; © Theowulf Maehl/zefa/CORBIS, pp. 5 (second from left), 20; © Sam Abell/National Geographic Society Image Collection, pp. 5 (center), 33; © Doug Perrine/SeaPics.com, pp. 5 (second from right), 45 (top), 48; © Dennis O'Clair/Stone/Getty Images, pp. 5 (right), 53; Guide Dogs for the Blind, www.guidedogs.com, pp. 6, 11 (top), 12 (both), 13; AP Photo/David Karp, p. 7; AP Photo/John Labriola, File, p. 8; AP Photo/Suzanne Plunkett, p. 10; AP Photo/Daniel Hulshizer, p. 11 (bottom); AP Photo/Pete Barreras, p. 14; AP Photo/WLS-TV, p. 15; © John Zich/Time & Life Pictures/Getty Images, p. 16; © Michael Nichols/National Geographic/Getty Images, p. 17; AP Photo/Charles Rex Arbogast, p. 18; AP Photo/Sayyid Azim, p. 19 (both); © APN/Warren Buckland, p. 22; © Skip Jeffery Photography, pp. 23, 37; AP Photo/Dave Martin, p. 25; © age fotostock/SuperStock, p. 26; AP Photo/LM Otero, p. 27; © Gary W. Carter/CORBIS, p. 29; © Barry Williams/Getty Images, p. 30; © SIU/Visuals Unlimited, p. 35; AP Photo/Don Ryan, pp. 36, 38; © Greg Kozawa, p. 39; © Dr. Fred Hossler/Visuals Unlimited, p. 41; © Barnaby Hall/Photonica/Getty Images, p. 43; © Florian Graner/SeaPics.com, p. 45 (bottom); © Paul A. Souders/CORBIS, p. 46; Courtesy of Sue Howes, p. 49; Official U.S. Navy Photograph, p. 51; Mike Lingenfelter & David Frei, pp. 55, 56, 57; Courtesy of Helping Hands, p. 59 (top).

Front Cover: © Mike Perry/Minden Pictures/Getty Images (background); © APN/Mark Mitchell (top); AP Photo/Don Ryan (second from top); AP Photo/WLS-TV (second from bottom); AP Photo/Tina Fineberg (bottom).